Table of Contents

Rourke
Educational Media
rourkeeducationalmedia.com

A Division of
Carson
Dellosa
Education

Can you find these words?

found

leadership

respect

symbol

Washington Monument

A **symbol** stands for an idea.

The Washington Monument is a symbol of **respect**.

It is a symbol of thanks.

The monument is in Washington, D.C.

PACIFIC OCEAN

WASHINGTON
OREGON
IDAHO
MONTANA
WYOMING
NORTH DAKOTA
SOUTH DAKOTA
MINNESOTA
WISCONSIN
MICHIGAN
NEVADA
UTAH
COLORADO
NEBRASKA
IOWA
ILLINOIS
INDIANA
OHIO
CALIFORNIA
ARIZONA
NEW MEXICO
KANSAS
MISSOURI
KENTUCKY
WEST VIRGINIA
VIRGINIA
PENNSYLVANIA
OKLAHOMA
ARKANSAS
TENNESSEE
NORTH CAROLINA
SOUTH CAROLINA
TEXAS
LOUISIANA
MISSISSIPPI
ALABAMA
GEORGIA
FLORIDA
NEW HAMPSHIRE
VERMONT
MAINE
NEW YORK
MASSACHUSETTS
RHODE ISLAND
CONNECTICUT
NEW JERSEY
DELAWARE
WASHINGTON D.C.
ATLANTIC OCEAN
GULF OF MEXICO
UNITED STATES OF AMERICA
ALASKA
HAWAII

WASHINGTON D.C.

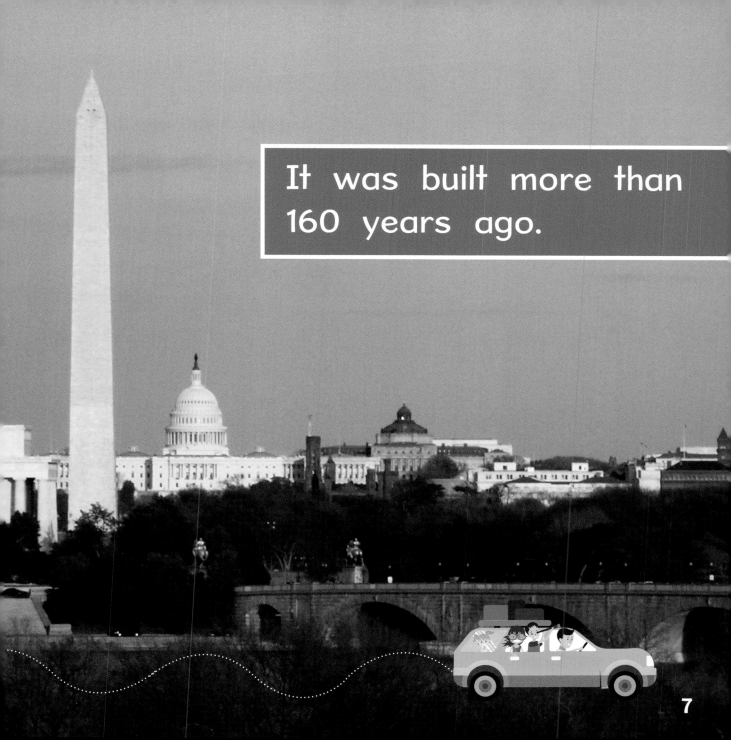

It was built more than 160 years ago.

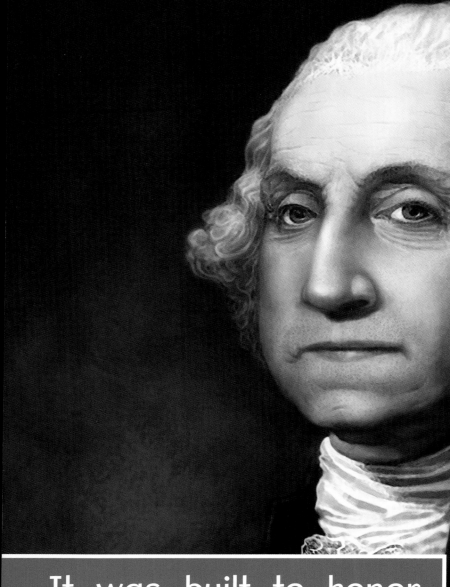

It was built to honor George Washington.

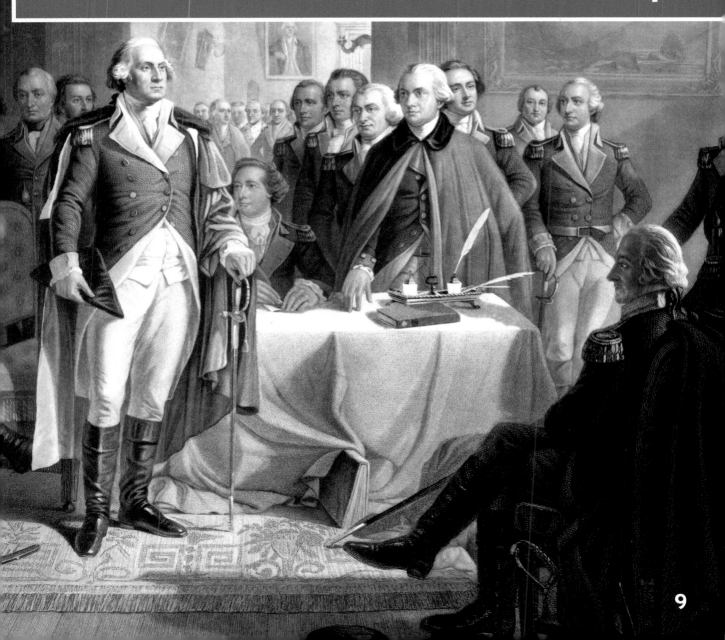

It was built to honor his **leadership.**

George Washington helped **found** the United States.

GEORGE WASHINGTON,

FIRST PRESIDENT OF THE UNITED STATES.

From the Original Series painted by Stuart
for the Mess.rs Doggett of Boston

He became its first president.

You can visit the monument.
You can go inside.

You can go all the way to the top!

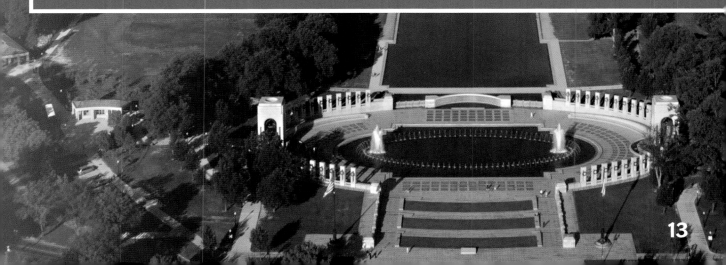

Did you find these words?

George Washington helped **found** the United States.

It was built to honor his **leadership**.

The Washington Monument is a symbol of **respect**.

A **symbol** stands for an idea.

Photo Glossary

 **found** (found): To establish something, such as a school, a business, or a country.

 **leadership** (leed-UR-ship): The action of leading a group of people.

 **respect** (ri-SPEKT): A feeling of admiration or high regard for someone or something.

 **symbol** (SIM-buhl): A design or object that stands for, suggests, or represents something else.

15

Index

About the Author

K.A. Robertson is a writer and editor who enjoys learning about the history of the United States. She thinks George Washington is a very interesting person to read about!

www.rourkeeducationalmedia.com

PHOTO CREDITS: Cover: ©drnadig; Pg 2, 10, 14, 15 ©Willard; Pg 2, 3, 14, 15 ©RichVintage; Pg 2, 4, 14, 15 ©flownaksala; Pg 2, 9, 14, 15 ©kreicher; Pg 5 ©Sean Pavone; Pg 6 ©KenHoward; Pg 8 ©joecicak; Pg 10 ©Library of Congress; Pg 11 ©Wiki; Pg 12 ©ValeStock; Pg 13 ©Library of Congress

Edited by: Kim Thompson
Cover and interior design by: Kathy Walsh

Library of Congress PCN Data
Washington Monument / K.A. Robertson
(Visiting U.S. Symbols)
ISBN 978-1-73160-570-2 (hard cover)(alk. paper)
ISBN 978-1-73160-404-0 (soft cover)
ISBN 978-1-73160-619-8 (e-Book)
ISBN 978-1-73160-645-7 (ePub)
Library of Congress Control Number: 2018967353

Printed in the United States of America,
North Mankato, Minnesota